Let's Play
TAG!

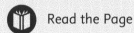 Read the Page

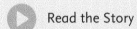 Read the Story

 Game

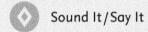 Sound It / Say It

Repeat

Stop

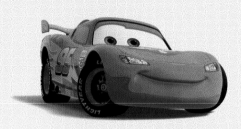

Get-Ready Words

cheer	rival
famous	The Queen
fierce	tow truck
Piston Cup	trophy
pit crew	World Grand Prix

Disney · PIXAR
Cars

Racing Adventures

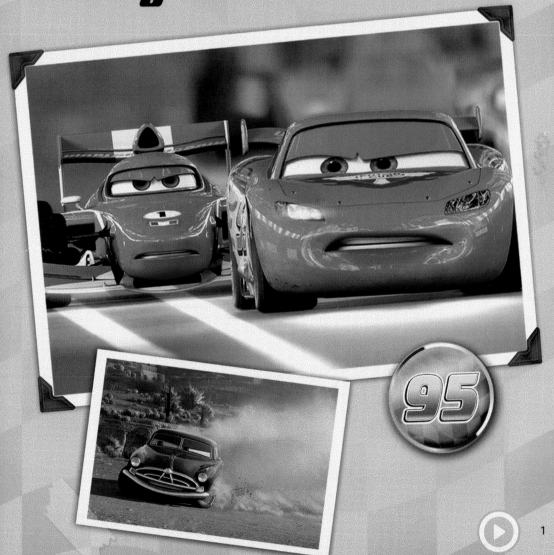

95

Lightning

 Lightning McQueen wanted to be a famous race car.

"I'll win the Piston Cup!"
Lightning said.

His first big race was the Dinoco 400. He raced with Chick Hicks and The King. They finished at the same time.

"No way!" Lightning thought.

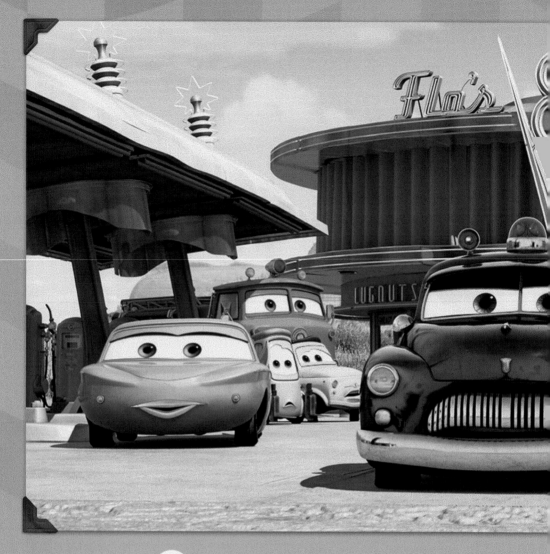

Lightning left for the next race.
He came to a town. It was
Radiator Springs.

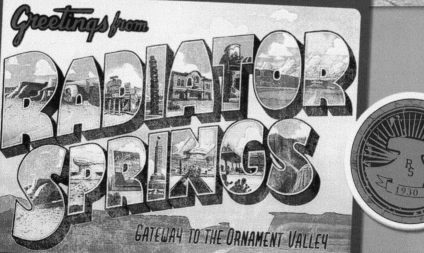

Greetings from

RADIATOR SPRINGS

GATEWAY TO THE ORNAMENT VALLEY

Lightning met Mater,
the tow truck.

When Lightning needed help,
Mater gave him a tow.

HORNET

Soon, Lightning
met Doc Hudson.
They raced in a dirt race.
Lightning thought this would be easy.
But he lost. Lightning still had a lot
to learn.

No one knew that Doc had been a famous
race car. Doc had
won the Piston Cup
three times!

PISTON
CUP

Third Piston Cup Win!

HUDSON HORNET
CHAMPION FOR ALL TIME

 Lightning went to the final Piston Cup race. His friends cheered for him. Lightning helped The King. This made Lightning lose the race.

But he was
happy. He had
made a lot of
new friends.

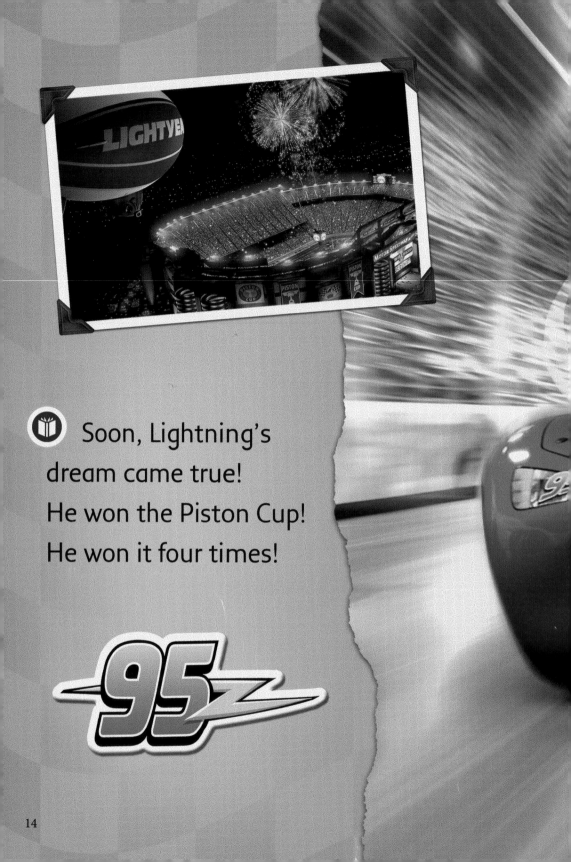

Soon, Lightning's dream came true! He won the Piston Cup! He won it four times!

WORLD grand prix

Lightning raced in the World Grand Prix. He raced with cars from all over the world!

The first race
was in Japan.

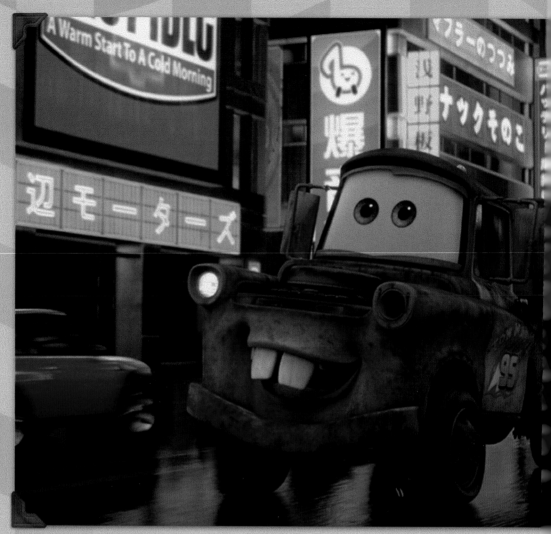

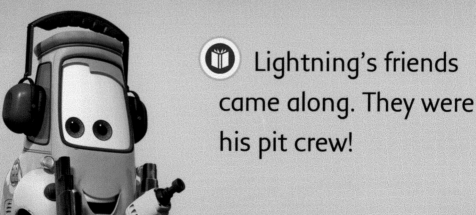

Lightning's friends came along. They were his pit crew!

The next race was in Italy.
Francesco was a fierce rival.

Lightning wanted to beat him!

The third race was in London.
Lightning met the Queen of England.

Lightning was now a world famous
race car. He won lots of trophies.

Even better, he had made lots of
good friends.

Words You're Learning

Short Vowels

Short a Words	Short e Words	Short i Words	Short o Words	Short u Words
at	help	him	Doc	but
Grand	left	pit	lost	Cup
had	next	this	lot	truck
that	went	win		
	when	with		

Long Vowels

Long a Words	Long e Words	Long i Words	Long o Words	Long u/oo Words
came	be	time	no	crew
gave	beat		tow	knew
made	dream			soon
race	he			true
same	three			

Sight Words

another	from	the	were
been	learn	they	won
four	one	thought	world
friends	said	was	would